D0888517

Char TerBeest, *text*
Rhonda Nass, *illustrations*

gifts from the earth
A BASKETMAKER'S FIELD GUIDE TO MIDWEST BOTANICALS

Gifts from the Earth
Copyright 1988

Char TerBeest , *text*
Wild Willow Press
P.O. Box 438
Baraboo, Wisconsin 53913

Rhonda Nass, *illustrations*
Ampersand
P.O. Box 97
Cross Plains, Wisconsin 53528

Edited by Pat Mantsch and Jane Whitney

Cover Painting: acrylic on canvas, Rhonda Nass, 1988

Back Cover Photo: Dan Zenker

ISBN 0-9614795-1-5
L.O.C. 88-050438

DEDICATION

Lovingly dedicated
to my Mother and Father
Helen and Russell TerBeest
for their teachings about life
and respect for the land.
They believed in my dreams.

ACKNOWLEDGMENTS

Many Midwest basketmakers helped supply valuable "gathering secrets" in order for me to complete this book. Their openness, encouragement, cooperation and friendship helped see this project through. Their energy and dedication to their craft is greatly admired and appreciated; with education comes understanding and acceptance.

Thanks for your sharing!

Jim Bennett, Michigan
Jo Campbell-Amsler, Iowa
Fran Cheney, Wisconsin
Kathleen Crombie, Michigan
John Hayes, Indiana
Holiday Hayes, Indiana
Cindy Nishimura, Ohio

Cliff Nishimura, Ohio
Kathy Rehling, Ohio
Joanna Schanz, Iowa
Dave Schmidt, Iowa
Kathy Schmidt, Iowa
Sandy Whalen, Michigan
Sandy Webster, Michigan

Mention should be made of all my friends who allowed me to rummage through their "nature book" libraries. Without the use of their precious books, much of this information would not have been discovered.

Also, deep and sincere gratitude is extended to the talented illustrator, Rhonda Nass. Magic emerges through her fingers, and lines turn into realistic living plants you can almost smell.

Char TerBeest

Thank you, Lord, for giving me a talent I thoroughly enjoy practicing as I give it back to you...and for providing this beautiful wood and marsh (source material) at our back door.

Thank you, Rick, for being willing to work yourself silly so we could live on your income as I was focusing on *Gifts from the Earth*...and for liking peanut butter sandwiches.

Thank you, family and friends, for supplying what I needed in the way of prayers, prods, patience and patronage for the "the '87–'88 project."

Thank you, former authors, educators, and illustrators (bibliography) for making it possible to accurately observe and depict the species represented in these pages. Thank you, Ray and Suzie, for passing on your excitement and appreciation of nature as I drew my first botanical illustrations for your '81 text. Hopefully that same respect will be passed on to the "listeners and lookers" of *Gifts from the Earth.*

And thank you, Char, for being steadfast to follow through on your initial idea to do *Gifts from the Earth,* for sharing your fine weaving skills as both artist and teacher, and for overall being a joy to work with. The whole process has been a pleasure for me.

Rhonda Nass

CONTENTS

INTRODUCTION

As two individuals we each have a unique intent for *Gifts from the Earth*. (Char writes with gatherers, basketmakers and artists in mind; she shares her intimacy with and knowledge of the materials in a way that only a gatherer could. Rhonda illustrates [accompanied by captions] with artists and nature enthusiasts in mind.) We hope together we contribute to the love and appreciation we all have as basketmakers, artists or naturalists for the natural world which surrounds us.

"Gatherers are a unique class of basketmaker. They are givers and takers and sharers. They see baskets everywhere—on vine-covered houses, willow-lined wetlands and growing around tree trunks. They feel a responsibility for the land and realize in taking care of the earth, she takes care of and nurtures them.

We hope for you, as a reader of Gifts..., *that a new way of "seeing" emerges. By stepping into basketing as a gatherer, life will appear different. That looking and wondering and experimenting will finally lead to beauty and understanding.*

Gifts...*was a joy to research and write. Many friends shared their vast experiences so that the novice could understand, enjoy and "see" the beauty of the land. Other gatherers may use different methods of preparing and storing the botanicals, but these are some that are helpful."**

Char TerBeest

"At any age, we can always use our kindergarten teacher's advice: "Always leave the room better than you find it." As people who enjoy and borrow from nature, whether as gatherers or artists, we try to practice this principle in practical ways (asking permission before trespassing, collecting trash as we wander and gather, and responsibly cutting for the future health of the plants if we collect**). We are grateful to preserve what we now enjoy.

We hope Gifts from the Earth *will help each of us see, hear, feel and respect our natural world with a deeper gratitude for it."*

Rhonda Nass

As two educators we have tried to make this book educational, accurate in content, and a pleasure to read. As two artists we have tried to make *Gifts from the Earth* as "easy on the eyes" as the beautiful natural world we are representing.

We hope you enjoy *Gifts from the Earth*.

*Use the resources around you—freezers, ovens, refrigerators, and microwave oven. All are convenient and make the basketmaker's tasks easier and more productive.

**Cutting 1/4" above the plant node with clean cuts will keep the healthy plant less vulnerable to disease, decay or insects. Also before cutting, it is wise to check with your Department of Natural Resources to spot protected botanicals.

WILLOW and OTHER TWIGS

dogwood
forsythia
willow

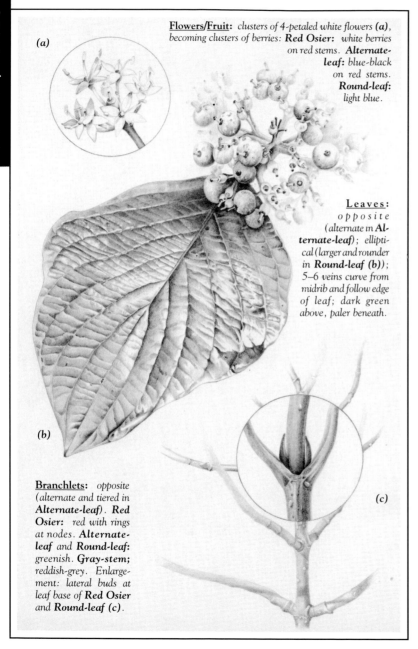

Flowers/Fruit: *clusters of 4-petaled white flowers* **(a)**, *becoming clusters of berries:* **Red Osier:** *white berries on red stems.* **Alternate-leaf:** *blue-black on red stems.* **Round-leaf:** *light blue.*

(a)

Leaves: *opposite (alternate in* **Alternate-leaf***); elliptical (larger and rounder in* **Round-leaf (b)***); 5–6 veins curve from midrib and follow edge of leaf; dark green above, paler beneath.*

(b)

(c)

Branchlets: *opposite (alternate and tiered in* **Alternate-leaf***).* **Red Osier:** *red with rings at nodes.* **Alternate-leaf** *and* **Round-leaf:** *greenish.* **Gray-stem:** *reddish-grey. Enlargement: lateral buds at leaf base of* **Red Osier** *and* **Round-leaf (c).**

dogwood
CORNUS
**Alternate-leaf, Gray-stem
Red Osier, Round-leaf**

Description: Red Osier Dogwood is a shrub that may grow ten feet or more. The branches are a brilliant red in the winter making a breathtaking contrast against the stark white of the snow. Chlorophyll returns to the branches in summer, restoring its greenness. The leaves are elliptical or ovate, are not toothed, with strong veining emerging from the mid-leafstalk. The white berries mature in late summer, making dogwood thickets a haven for many birds. A yellow-barked variety is also available.

Habitat: Dogwood will grow next to the willow in wet or marshy areas. Many people plant dogwood in their yards.

Gathered: The young shoots (suckers) growing under the branches make the best weavers and can be gathered from November to April. In the summer the shoots are generally green and brittle. The larger branches can be formed into handles and rims.

Storage: For the best storage of dogwood, tie into bundles, place in plastic bags and freeze to preserve the bark. If dried and later soaked, the bark rubs or falls off because the twig will shrink more than the bark.

Preparation: Dogwood must thaw four to six hours before using, or it can be used soon after it is gathered.

Comments: The bark of **Red Osier Dogwood** may turn a dark ox blood red when dry. Gathering during early spring may yield a brighter, longer lasting red color after the branch dries.

Folklore: **Red Osier Dogwood** was used by Native Americans for its many healing properties. An old spiritual poem parallels the redness of the branches in spring to the blood shed to save mankind from sin.

Description: Forsythia is a twiggy bush grown domestically in most parts of the United States. The bush can reach heights of ten feet. The leaves are on stalks, are oblong shaped, and toothed. Its flowers are bright yellow, grow in clusters and blossom in the spring. The flowers have four lobes and may bloom with the unfolding of the leaves.

forsythia
FORSYTHIA
Greenstem, Weeping

Habitat: Forsythia is an extremely hardy bush and can grow in almost any soil. It can be seen growing in yards and gardens. Sometimes it can be found in abandoned fields.

Gathered: The bush can be gathered almost any time of the year. The best gathering time is after the leaves fall off or before it flowers.

Storage: This plant is best used immediately after gathering. The author would not recommend storing this bush.

Preparation: Use soon after gathering. Cover with plastic to keep as much dry air away from the plant as possible. When gathering in summer, the leaves must be removed.

Comments: Forsythia is best used for a more randomly woven basket because of its limited flexibility. If planting in the yard, prune the plant after it flowers and cut it close to the ground.

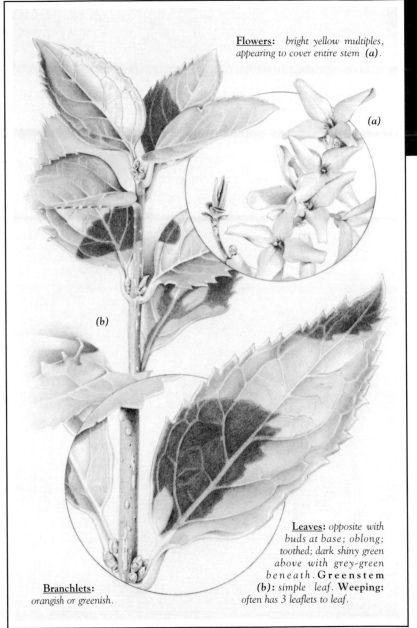

Flowers: bright yellow multiples, appearing to cover entire stem (a).

(a)

(b)

Leaves: opposite with buds at base; oblong; toothed; dark shiny green above with grey-green beneath. Greenstem (b): simple leaf. Weeping: often has 3 leaflets to leaf.

Branchlets: *orangish or greenish.*

11

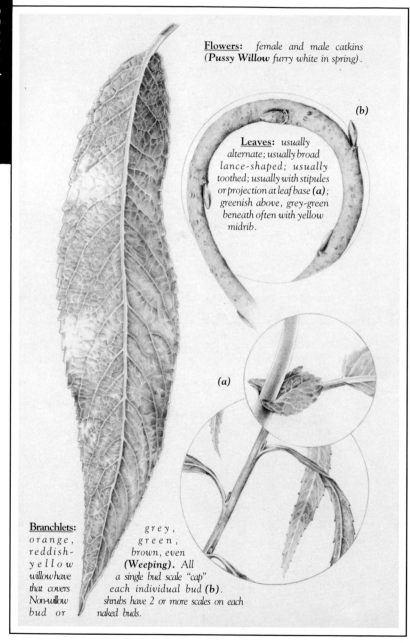

Flowers: *female and male catkins* (**Pussy Willow** *furry white in spring*).

(b)

Leaves: *usually alternate; usually broad lance-shaped; usually toothed; usually with stipules or projection at leaf base (a); greenish above, grey-green beneath often with yellow midrib.*

(a)

Branchlets: *orange, reddish-yellow willow have that covers Non-willow bud or*

*grey, green, brown, even (**Weeping**). All a single bud scale "cap" each individual bud (b). shrubs have 2 or more scales on each naked buds.*

willow
SALIX

Description: Willow may vary in height and size. Most willow will grow from one foot to seven feet in one year's growth period. As a tree or shrub, it will seldom reach heights over 20 feet (except **Weeping Willow** [*salix babylonia*] which is an inferior material because as it dries this species becomes brittle and fragile). Catkins develop on the branches in spring. New shoots grow as a single twig and may vary in color from a reddish brown to bright green or gray.

Habitat: Willow will generally grow in thickets near water, seldom in it. The best willow grows in wetlands and marshes. Willow has even been seen growing between cracks in a rock quarry. Willow is a hardy shrub/tree and can be easily grown in yards and gardens.

Gathered: Gather willow in the fall after the leaves have fallen off the branch and before it begins to bud out in spring (between November and April is the best gathering time in Wisconsin). Each region has different growing seasons, so the best harvesting time will vary from state to state. Willow can be gathered in the spring or summer, but at these times willow is in a "green" stage and is not flexible.

Storage: Tie gathered willow into bundles for freezing, and place in plastic bags. When drying, twigs can be sorted according to size and height, loosely stacked, and bundled. Store in a dry place protected from the sun and wind.

Preparation: Let willow thaw four to six hours after removing it from the freezer. Dried willow must be soaked in water. Add one cup of fabric softener to the water to improve flexibility and to keep the willow smelling fresh. A general rule of thumb: soak withies one day for each foot-length of the branch. A "kiddie pool", animal watering tank, and even a canoe work well for the soaking willow.

Comments: There is more shrinkage in fresh or frozen willow than in soaked willow. Willow has much strength and "spirit". Willow is one of the first trees to bud out in the spring and it will keep its leaves long after the first snow of winter.

Folklore: Willow has long been the subject of many tales and lore. Magic wands are made from willow and mothers have been heard telling their children to stay away from the willows. Because of its composition, willow has been used for ancient medicines and rituals. The catkins of willow were once used as an aphrodisiac. A forked willow branch is sometimes used as a dowsing stick to find water.

BARK

basswood
birch
hickory
poplar

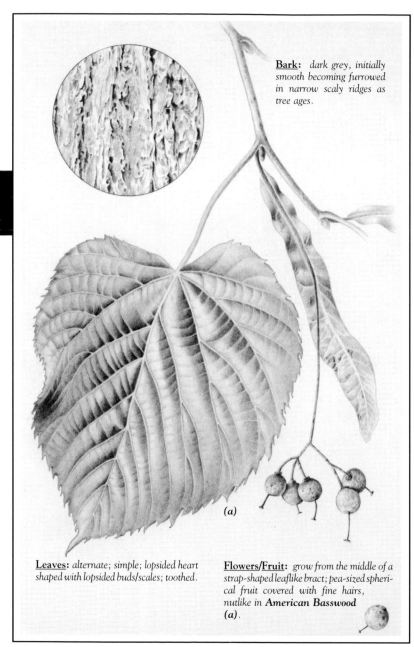

Bark: *dark grey, initially smooth becoming furrowed in narrow scaly ridges as tree ages.*

(a)

Leaves: *alternate; simple; lopsided heart shaped with lopsided buds/scales; toothed.*

Flowers/Fruit: *grow from the middle of a strap-shaped leaflike bract; pea-sized spherical fruit covered with fine hairs, nutlike in* **American Basswood** *(a).*

basswood
TILIA

also known as **linden: American**

Description: Basswood, oftentimes called linden, is a large tree, 70 feet or more, with a dense crown and drooping branches. The leaves are very large, sometimes six inches long, are heartshaped and are coarsely saw-toothed. The dark gray bark is quite smooth in a young tree, turning into deep furrows as the tree ages. It produces a small nut-like fruit which matures in late summer.

Habitat: Basswood will grow in moist valleys. It can be successfully planted for a shade tree.

Gathered: The tree must first be cut down. Look for young saplings three to five inches in diameter. Spring is generally the best time to collect basswood. The bark may be stripped off in vertical strips. The poles can be aged and used as firewood.

Storage: Store the bark strips in a well-ventilated, cool, dry place. To prevent infestation, keep it off the floor and away from bugs and other pests.

Preparation: Basswood bark can be soaked in water or steamed to make it more flexible. The bark can also be used fresh. Both the inner and outer bark can be utilized. If the basketmaker wishes to make cordage, the inner basswood bark is soaked in water for 7–14 days. This is called "retting." It softens the tissues so the inner fiber will pull apart into small strips. These strips can be used singly or twisted together into cordage. Refer to Carol and Dan Hart's book, *Natural Basketry*, for more detailed information covering basswood.

Comments: Basswood trees are very diverse and can be used in many phases of basketmaking. The tree blooms in early spring. Many woodcarvers and whittlers choose basswood because the wood has an even grain and is quite soft.

Description: This showy forest tree will grow to heights of 70 feet. The leaf is ovate and is a dull green. It has a strong mid-vein and is heavily toothed. Birch bark appears creamy white or even silver. Birch sometimes has a shredded, layered appearance and long horizontal lines. In the fall the small (one half to two inch) cones mature.

birch
BETULA
Gray, Paper

Habitat: Birch can be found in moist uplands, lake shores and river banks. In the far northern parts of the Midwest, it can be found growing in pure stands. The cooler the climate, the thicker the birch bark.

Gathered: The best time to gather birch is late spring, early summer or late fall. If the tree is frozen, it is almost impossible to remove the bark. Never take bark from a living tree; this will kill the tree. Take bark from an already fallen tree or a tree may be cut down. (For easier gathering take a friend to help strip the bark.) Cut the bark down the middle of the trunk and carefully pull it off. Remove all debris from the inner and outer bark. Oftentimes one can find an area being logged and, with permission, can remove bark from already downed trees.

Storage: If gathering fresh bark, place it between two plywood boards and C-clamp it together. Dry bark can be stacked and stored in a cool, dry place, free from pests and bugs.

Preparation: Freshly gathered bark can be used immediately. It can be cut into strips, folded, lashed or sewn together. Dried bark can be soaked or steamed for more flexibility. A steam iron can be a useful tool when working with bark.

Comments: Birch bark is a rapidly growing, short-lived tree. Oftentimes toothpicks, clothespins and spools are made from birch. If adding "trash" (fungus, lichens, etc.) to a basket, place the piece to be used in the microwave or place in a plastic bag with a pest strip for a few days. This will destroy any bugs still living in the bark.

Folklore: **Paper Birch** is oftentimes called "Canoe Birch." Far Northern Native Americans sewed birch to a frame of white cedar with tamarack roots and sealed the seams with fir resin. Birch bark was even ground into flour to make bread. Layers of birch strips were added to stew as noodles. The sap was tapped and boiled down into syrup, but it is only half as sweet as the maple variety.

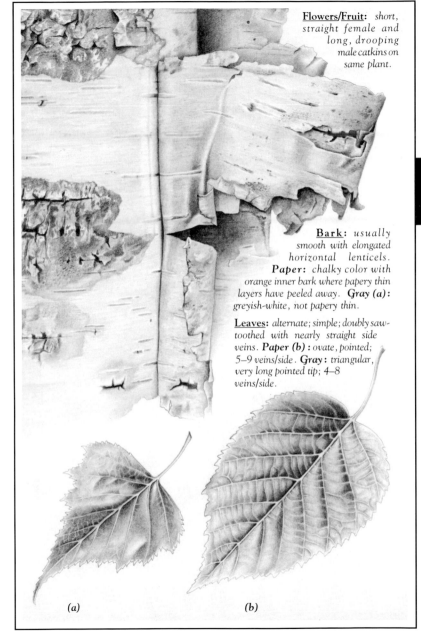

Flowers/Fruit: *short, straight female and long, drooping male catkins on same plant.*

Bark: *usually smooth with elongated horizontal lenticels.* **Paper:** *chalky color with orange inner bark where papery thin layers have peeled away.* **Gray (a):** *greyish-white, not papery thin.*

Leaves: *alternate; simple; doubly saw-toothed with nearly straight side veins.* **Paper (b):** *ovate, pointed; 5–9 veins/side.* **Gray:** *triangular, very long pointed tip; 4–8 veins/side.*

(a) *(b)*

Fruit: *thick husk of nut splits (4 parts) to base when ripe.*
Shagbark (a): *fruit 1¼–2½" yellow-green husk turning to black, then splitting to release whitish shell with elliptical edible seed within.* **Shellbark:** *thick-shelled nut can be as large as 2" long.*

Leaves: *mostly alternate; pinnately compound with larger terminal leaflet; finely toothed.*

Shagbark (c): *usually 5, 3–7" ovate leaflets on 8–14" leaf.*
Shellbark: *usually 7–9 broadly lance-shaped leaflets on 12–20" leaf.*

(a)

(b)

Note leaf stalk attachment with bud (b).

(c)

Bark: *light grey; rough plated with curved, loosely attached strips (at middle in* **Shagbark (d)***).*

(d)

hickory
CARYA
Shagbark, Shellbark

Description: Hickory trees grow to heights of 100 feet. The leaves are a yellow-green color and are pinnately compound with five to seven leaflets on each stalk. The leaf is toothed. This tree can live to 250 years and will not bear fruit until it is about 80 years old. The fruit is a nut. It is round with four to six grooves and is edible. The bark of **Shagbark Hickory** is gray and in older trees will grow in loose-hanging strips, giving the trunk a shaggy appearance. Twigs of **Shellbark** are pale orange.

Habitat: Hickory trees grow throughout North America in moist valleys, uplands, and in mixed hardwood forests.

Gathered: Bark should be gathered from young trees during the spring of the year. The tree will have to be cut down, and the bark removed with a knife. The leftover "poles" can be used in fireplaces and stoves after being properly dried .

Storage: Store bark strips in a cool, dry place to prevent bark from molding. It should be kept off the floor and away from insects.

Preparation: To use hickory bark, soak in hot water until pliable. Drain and cut into strips for weaving or sew it together. The wood can also be split and used as splints. Refer to "TREES/oak" for more information.

Comments: Hickory is an extremely hard wood; baseball bats are made from hickory. Hickory is also used for smoking meat.

Folklore: Native Americans pounded the shell of the nut for a powder that, when mixed with water, made a milky liquor. General Andrew Jackson was nicknamed "Old Hickory" because he was "tough as hickory" to deal with.

Description: The poplar family can include **Aspen, Cottonwood,** and **Balsam.** This tree is a rapid grower and will be one of the first to appear on land after a forest fire. It will reach heights of 80 feet. The shiny leaf is often heart-shaped, toothed, with a long leafstalk. The bark is fairly smooth and gray to silver-gray. The male and female flowers grow on separate trees.

poplar
POPULUS
Bigtooth Poplar, Cottonwood, Quaking Aspen

Habitat: Poplars grow in moist woodlands, borders of fields, and roadsides.

Gathered: Gather the bark from young trees two to six inches in diameter. The saplings must be cut down, slit along the center of the trunk and the bark removed. The best time to gather poplar bark is in the spring of the year. The poles can be used for firewood after they have been properly dried.

Storage: The bark can be placed between two large boards and C-clamped together. It can also be piled in a cool, dry, well-ventilated place, off the floor away from bugs and pests.

Preparation: Poplar bark can be cut into strips and woven. Later, pieces can be scored and sewn together. Barks can be mixed together for interesting effects. The dried bark should be soaked in water or steamed to make it more flexible. Poplars can also be made into splints.

Comments: Poplars first grew in Europe and were introduced in North America during colonial days. They make terrific shade trees. In the fall the leaves are a bright mass of gold.

Folklore: Poplars have salicin, an active ingredient found in aspirin. Farmers have been heard telling their children, "If you see the wind showing the silvery backs of poplar leaves, rain is certain to be on its way."

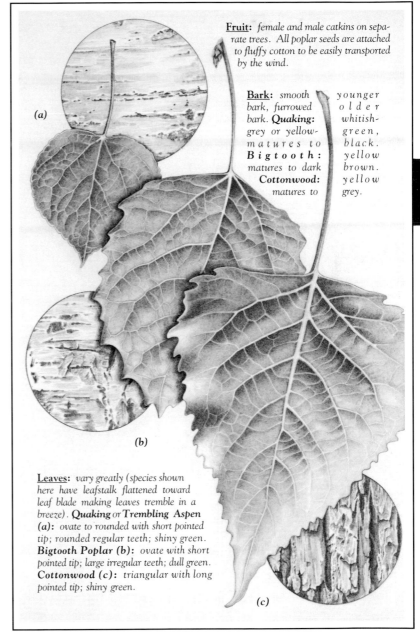

Fruit: *female and male catkins on separate trees. All poplar seeds are attached to fluffy cotton to be easily transported by the wind.*

Bark: *smooth bark, furrowed bark.* **Quaking:** *grey or yellow-matures to* **Bigtooth:** *matures to dark* **Cottonwood:** *matures to* | *younger older whitish-green, black. yellow brown. yellow grey.*

BARK

Leaves: *vary greatly (species shown here have leafstalk flattened toward leaf blade making leaves tremble in a breeze).* **Quaking** *or* **Trembling Aspen (a):** *ovate to rounded with short pointed tip; rounded regular teeth; shiny green.* **Bigtooth Poplar (b):** *ovate with short pointed tip; large irregular teeth; dull green.* **Cottonwood (c):** *triangular with long pointed tip; shiny green.*

VINES
bittersweet
grape
honeysuckle
ivy
morning glory
virginia creeper
wisteria

Description: Bittersweet is a woody, twining vine growing 30-foot runners. The leaf is ovate and finely serrated. The vine is gray and will bear clusters of brilliant red berries after its orange or yellow capsules split open. The berries will appear in the fall.

bittersweet
CELASTRUS
American, Oriental

Habitat: The vine has escaped from cultivation and grows in thickets, along fences, woods, and river banks.

Gathered: Collect bittersweet vines preferably in the fall after the first frost. The leaves will have fallen off and the vine will have reached its full year's growth. This creeper can also be gathered year-round.

Storage: Store the coiled vines in a cool, dry place, off the floor and away from pests and bugs.

Preparation: Bittersweet is best used soon after collecting. The vine can be boiled in water or steamed to soften. Soaking the vine can cause deterioration of this botanical so should not be processed this way.

Comments: Bittersweet must have a male and female plant close to each other to produce berries. The berries should not be eaten because of their poisonous ingredients.

Flowers/Fruit: *fruit with spherical outside case, berry within.* **Oriental (a):** *yellow case, red berry; flowers and fruit appearing along stem (axillary).* **American (b):** *orange case, red berry; flowers and fruit appearing at end of stems (terminal).*

(a)

Note bark of vines.

Leaves: *alternate; simple; finely serrated; buds projecting from stems at right angles; twining vines (no tendrils).* **Oriental (c)** *has more rounded leaves and teeth.*

(b)

(c)

VINES

Stems: *All grapes have brown pith. Tendrils are opposite the leaves or buds and are usually forked. Stems (vines) appear natural and stripped.*

(a)

Leaves: *alternate; simple; usually lobed with very sharp teeth; highly veined; hairy beneath (**Summer** and **Fox** are most common; these have pale undersides early in season, rusty later in season).*

Flowers/ Fruit: *spherical fruit in clusters usually with a bloom* **Summer (a):** *dark blue, purple, black.* **Fox:** *dark blue, black, red, brown, green.*

grape
VITIS
Fox, Summer

Description: Grapevine is a climbing botanical. The runners can grow many feet in one season. The vine has a woody stem with tendrils that aid in securing it to trees and fences. The broad-toothed leaf is heart-shaped, lobed with strong veining. The fruit grows in bunches from the vine and is used to make wines and jellies.

Habitat: Grapevine will grow almost anywhere. It can be found along roadsides, but it especially enjoys wooded areas, attaching itself to trees and shrubs. If not pruned, a tree covered with grapevine can die because of a lack of sun.

Gathered: Grapevine can be gathered year-round. Many basketmakers prefer to gather in the fall through winter and into spring when the leaves do not have to be removed from the vine.

Storage: Store coils in a cool, dry place or use soon after gathering. The vines can also be stripped of their leaves and frozen.

Preparation: Preparation of the vine will depend on the part of the plant the basketmaker decides to use. If using with the inner and outer bark, soak in water and weave. The vines should be soaked in water overnight. They can also be left out during a summer rain to make them more flexible. Grapevine can also be boiled in water for at least three hours. This will make the vines more pliable and can destroy any pest living in the plant. Another way of dealing with the pest, boring beetle, in the vine is by microwaving the vines or placing the completed piece in a plastic bag for a few days with a pest strip.

Comments: The tendrils of the vine can make it extremely rough to work with.

Folklore: The fruit of the vine has multiple uses. To add a delicate, acid flavor, many Middle Eastern recipes call for the use of grape leaves as a wrap for various foods.

Description:
Honeysuckle is a rampant woody climber, having runners growing 50 feet. The bluish-green leaf is oval and grows in pairs on the vine. The red flowers have yellow throats (some produce just yellow flowers) and grow in clusters. The flowers last a month or more and their sweet nectar attracts hummingbirds.

honeysuckle
LONICERA
Japanese, Limber, Trumpet or Coral,

Habitat: Honeysuckle grows in thickets or wooded areas. It can also be found in fields, waste places, and on fences.

Gathered: This vine can be gathered year-round. However, runners are longest in the fall, and the lack of leaves makes the basketmaker's job easier.

Storage: Store honeysuckle without leaves, in coils, in a cool, dry place. Keep them off the floor and away from pests and bugs.

Preparation: Many basketmakers boil the vines in water for three hours. Using a knife, rub the bark off the vine. The vine can then be coiled and dried. When ready to use, soak them in tepid water for 20 minutes. Honeysuckle will absorb dye readily.

Comments: Japanese Honeysuckle was introduced into the United States for groundcover and to prevent erosion along roadsides. Because of birds, this vine has been widely spread, threatening to overgrow entire eastern forests.

Folklore: Louise Riotte in her book, *Sleeping with a Sunflower*, discloses a secret honeysuckle recipe. Gather about a gallon of flowers and cover the blossoms with boiling water. Simmer for 20 minutes and strain out blossoms. Add a gallon of water, two and one half pounds of sugar, and two cups of white raisins. Add two sliced lemons, one package of yeast dissolved in a cup of water and two ginger roots. Let the covered mixture ferment for two weeks; strain it and put in a bottle. Let it sit for two months—then enjoy your tasty honeysuckle wine.

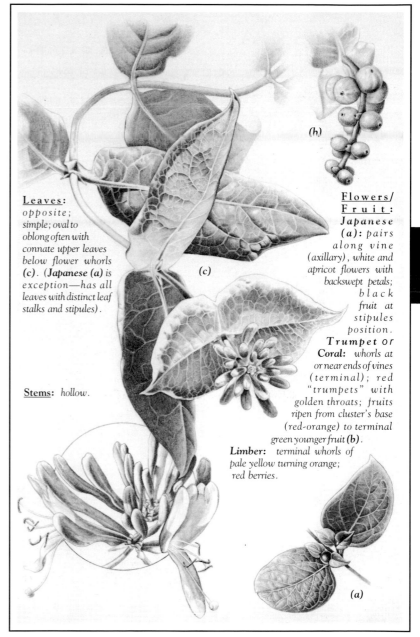

Leaves: *opposite; simple; oval to oblong often with connate upper leaves below flower whorls (c). (**Japanese (a)** is exception—has all leaves with distinct leaf stalks and stipules).*

Stems: *hollow.*

Flowers/Fruit: **Japanese (a):** *pairs along vine (axillary), white and apricot flowers with backswept petals; black fruit at stipules position.* **Trumpet or Coral:** *whorls at or near ends of vines (terminal); red "trumpets" with golden throats; fruits ripen from cluster's base (red-orange) to terminal green younger fruit (b).* **Limber:** *terminal whorls of pale yellow turning orange; red berries.*

VINES

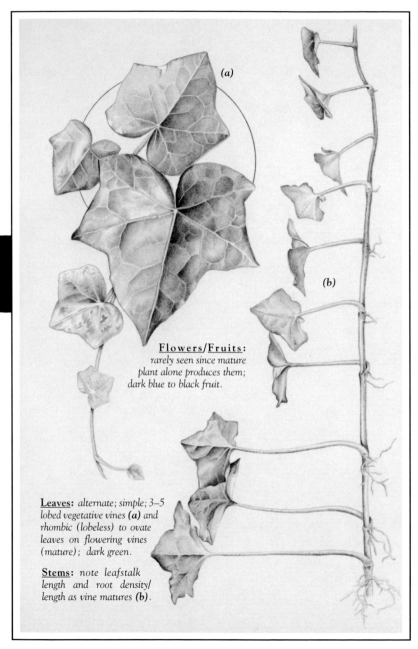

(a)

(b)

<u>Flowers</u>/<u>Fruits</u>:
*rarely seen since mature
plant alone produces them;
dark blue to black fruit.*

<u>Leaves</u>: *alternate; simple; 3–5
lobed vegetative vines (a) and
rhombic (lobeless) to ovate
leaves on flowering vines
(mature); dark green.*

<u>Stems</u>: *note leafstalk
length and root density/
length as vine matures (b).*

ivy
HEDERA
Boston, English

Description: Ivy is a hardy climbing vine reaching lengths of 100 feet. The glossy, alternating leaves may have three to five lobes per leaf. Ivy attaches itself to objects using aerial rootlets or adhesive pads.

Habitat: Many species of ivy grow in open woods. Most varieties of ivy have been planted and are seen growing along fences, up brick walls and houses. Ivy makes an excellent ground cover and thrives in shady areas.

Gathered: Basically, ivy can be gathered all year. The leaves must be removed from the vines during summer gathering.

Storage: Ivy vines should be wrapped in coils. Store dried vines in well-ventilated, dry areas. Store off the floor to prevent bug and pest infestations.

Preparation: Ivy is best used in its "green" form. The vine can be soaked in water overnight and should be well drained before weaving. Oversoaking can remove bark. Vines can also be steamed for 30-45 minutes. To keep it pliable, wrap vines in a damp towel.

Comments: Ivy became very popular for landscaping during the 1860's. The Victorian period saw an introduction of porches and verandas with ivy vines added for interesting effects.

Folklore: Some believe if one puts ivy under your pillow, your "true love's" face will appear in your dreams.

morning glory
IPOMOEA

Description: The morning glory family includes more than 500 species. The runners are slender and may grow 10 feet. The leaf is most often heart-shaped, but may have three lobes resembling an ivy. The leaves alternate on the vine and in midsummer flower into a funnel-shaped blossom. The showy flower may be white, lavender, blue, or rose in color.

Habitat: Morning glories will grow in almost any type of soil—generally in fields and disturbed areas.

Gathered: The vine should be gathered near the end of summer when it has reached its full growth.

Storage: During summer the leaves must be removed. Some weavers store it in plastic bags and place in the refrigerator or freezer. If the vine is dried, care must be taken when handling and storing.

Preparation: This vine is best used in its "green" form. However, there will be shrinkage. The best way to make this dried vine more pliable is by steaming it 30-45 minutes. Soaking may cause the vine to fall apart. Cording and braiding will add strength to the weavers. Because of the size of the runners it is a good material to use for making miniature baskets.

Comments: Wild morning glories have long been a nuisance for farmers. It will wind around cornstalks and beans, causing a lower yield. Edwin Spencer in his book, *All About Weeds*, writes:

> "Like snakes, those slender vines crawl up over the plants they select for their trellises, and soon the big Morning Glory leaves are shading the leaves of the plant, and soon after that those glorious flowers will be smiling on all the world like a big person obstructing the view of a small boy at the movies."

Folklore: *Ipomoea* is a Greek word meaning wormlike. The Aztecs use morning glory seeds as a psychoactive plant for wild visions and dreams.

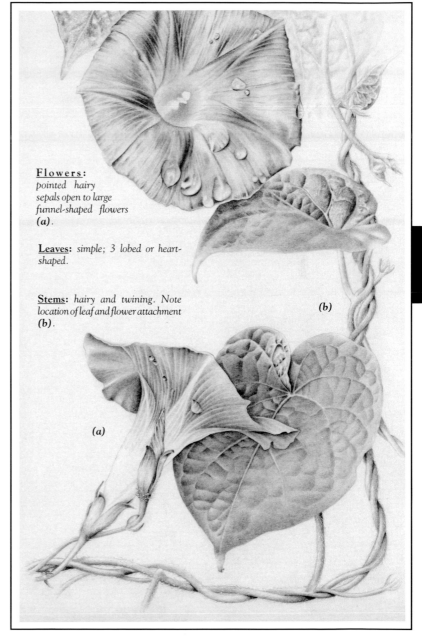

Flowers: pointed hairy sepals open to large funnel-shaped flowers **(a)**.

Leaves: simple; 3 lobed or heart-shaped.

Stems: hairy and twining. Note location of leaf and flower attachment **(b)**.

(b)

(a)

VINES

Note *Gifts from the Earth* cover painting.

Stems: *branched tendrils with adhesive disks (b) at tips; older stems have numerous aerial roots; white pith.*

Leaves: *alternate; palmately compound leaves of 5 leaflets; long leafstalks.*

Flowers/Fruit: *clusters of tiny green flowers; bluish-black berries (poisonous to humans, food for songbirds) on red stalks (a), glaucous.*

(b)

(a)

virginia creeper
PARTHENOCISSUS
also known as **woodbine**

Description: This vigorous creeper may grow to 50 feet. The foliage is dense with each stem developing five oblong leaflets. The runners are slender and somewhat woody. Small thread-like tendrils aid the vine in attaching to fences, walls, and trees. The fruit is small, dark blue and ripens in clusters. During the fall the leaves turn into a blaze of scarlet.

Habitat: Virginia creeper is extremely prolific and will grow readily in moist areas. It can generally be found growing along roadsides, fences, trees and buildings.

Gathered: The vine can be gathered all year, with fall being the most desirable time. The leaves have fallen off at this time, making less work for the basketmaker.

Storage: Virginia creeper should be stored in a cool, dry place. Wrap the vines into coils and store off the floor; this will prevent insect infestations.

Preparation: Virginia creeper can be used as soon as it is cut in the "green" stage. It can also be soaked in water overnight. Some weavers prefer steaming the vines.

Comments: Virginia creeper will turn a brilliant red in the fall and makes a beautiful ground cover. Poison ivy and Virginia creeper can look similar in appearance, especially when growing on a tree trunk. Poison ivy will have a reddish, shaggy hairlike root system growing from the vines.

Folklore: If one mistakes poison ivy for Virginia creeper, use this folk remedy. Make a lotion from jewel weed or wild touch-me-nots by boiling a potful of weeds in water until it is half the original amount. Strain out the juice and apply it to the exposed area. This lotion cannot be kept long. Freezing the liquid can be a positive way of preserving the lotion.

Description: The vine, wisteria, can reach lengths of 30-40 feet. This climber is extremely prolific. The leaves are alternate, almond-shaped, and compound. The drooping pealike flowers are usually violet, but are sometimes pink or white. They are found in clusters and grow only on mature plants.

Habitat: Wisteria is not a vine native to North America. People plant wisteria in their yards and gardens. However, run-away wisteria can be found growing along woods, climbing on trees, or on the ground. It is seldom found in the upper Midwest.

Gathered: This vine can be gathered all year. Early spring or fall is the best time to gather wisteria. During summer the leaves must be removed.

Storage: Store wisteria in coils after removing leaves in a dry, cool place. Store off the ground to keep insects from the vines.

Preparation: Wisteria can be used in the "green" stage. However, a little shrinkage should be expected. Dried coils of wisteria should be placed in warm water overnight. Drain well. Keep it damp for best weaving results. Some weavers prefer to first boil the materials to kill insect eggs.

Comments: Hardy wisteria can grow in the far North and can be ordered from seed catalogs.

Folklore: Wisteria was originally written as wistaria, and was intended to be written as such. Dr. Caspar Wistar, an American botanist, is this vine's namesake.

WISTERIA
American, Chinese, Japanese

Leaves: *alternate; pinnately compound, almond-shaped leaflets.* **Chinese:** *7–13 leaflets.* **American:** *9–15 leaflets (dark green mature leaves, but pinkish when young).* **Japanese (b):** *13–19 leaflets.*

(a)

(b)

Flowers/Fruit: *bluish-lavender flowers in drooping clusters that cover vine.* **Japanese (a):** *flowers open gradually from base to tip; long fruit pods are velvety.* **American:** *open approximately simultaneously; pods are smooth.*

(c)

Stems: *woody with spurs and lateral bud showing hornlike protuberancies (c) at each side.* (**American** *has more obvious lenticels and glossier bark.*)

LEAVES and GRASSES
cattail
daylily
flag
rush
sedge
sweetgrass

Description: The tall, bright green leaves of the cattail may grow six to ten feet in one season. The brown flower of the plant is a clublike spike. The top portion of the flower contains the male part of the plant with the larger, lower brown section containing the female parts.

cattail
TYPIIA

Habitat: Cattails will grow in any freshwater marsh or wetland throughout most of North America.

Gathered: Gather leaves of the cattail above the water line in the summer. The spikes can also be used in basketmaking. Collect spikes in late summer or early fall.

Storage: The leaves should be dried on a screen out of the sun. The sun can bleach the color out of the leaves. Store leaves in a cool, dry place. Cattail leaves also can be skirted. This is done with a tapestry needle threaded with heavy cording. Push the threaded needle through each leaf at the blunt end. They can then be tied in a circle and hung in a dry place.

Preparation: Cattails can be used in the "green" form. Much shrinkage should be expected when using green leaves. When using dried leaves, soak them in warm water for 30–60 minutes; drain well. The leaves and stalks can be split, then braided, twisted, or made into cordage for weaving.

Comments: Red-winged blackbirds make their nests in cattail marshes. They are furious protectors, so care must be taken while gathering during their nesting time.

Folklore: Another common name for cattails is bulrush. Moses was found floating in a basket among cattails. Native Americans have long feasted on cattails. Every part of this plant is edible. Early shoots can be eaten like asparagus. The young flowerspikes are boiled and eaten in salads. The pollen can even be collected and used as flour. Cattails are a real "smorgasbord" in the wild.

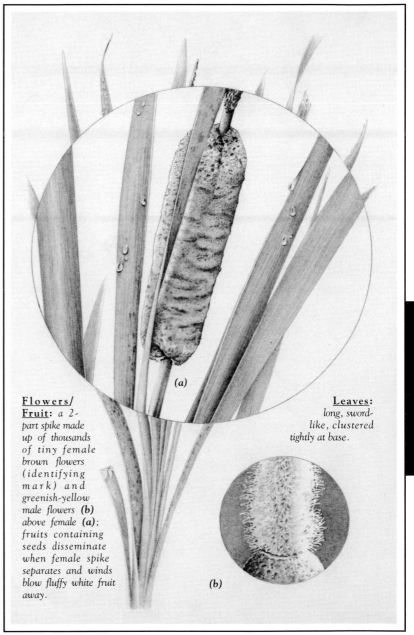

<u>Flowers/Fruit</u>: *a 2-part spike made up of thousands of tiny female brown flowers (identifying mark) and greenish-yellow male flowers* **(b)** *above female* **(a)**; *fruits containing seeds disseminate when female spike separates and winds blow fluffy white fruit away.*

<u>Leaves:</u> *long, sword-like, clustered tightly at base.*

(a)

(b)

LEAVES/GRASSES

(a)

Flowers: *trumpet or flowers borne at a time very short-lived— yellow burgundy and* *funnel-shaped, several at top of leafless stalk* **(a)**; *one/two days; orange, yellow* **(b)**.

(b)

Leaves: *somewhat droopy leaves, long and swordlike, clustered at base.*

daylily
HEMEROCALLIS

Description: Daylilies appear almost anywhere. They grow in densely clumped patches. The long yellow-green swordlike leaves bear a leafless, flowering stalk. In May and June it has a funnel-shaped flower. The plant may grow between two to four feet in one season.

Habitat: Daylilies are a garden escapee and can be found growing along roadsides, meadows and waste places.

Gathered: Lily leaves should be gathered in late summer, after it has reached its full growth. Gathering after the first frost will give the basketmaker a yellow, rust, or orange leaf. Always cut the leaves at the base of the plant. Never pull the plant out by the roots. Flower stalks can also be used for embellishments.

Storage: Leaves can be dried on a screen or tied in clumps and hung upside down on a beam or drying rack. If leaves are dried in the sun, the color will bleach out. By using a tapestry needle and a neutral-colored, durable cord, one can sew the leaves together at the base for skirting the botanicals.

Preparation: Soak the leaves in tepid water for an hour. Place them in a towel and keep them covered. Daylily leaves should not be re-soaked because this causes the fibers to deteriorate. Leaves can be used "green," but shrinkage should be expected.

Comments: Daylilies are a very old botanical. Many old family pictures of homesteads show how widely planted this lily was.

Folklore: The botanical's Greek name, *hemerocallis,* means "the fleeting pleasure of the day." The blooms last only one day, thus the name "daylily." All parts of the plant are edible. The tubers, flowers, and buds can be fried, baked, boiled, and even pickled, with the buds being the most tasty part of the plant.

Description: Flags are a showy botanical and are the country cousins of the garden iris. The yellow or blue-violet flowers rest on top of a robust stalk. The flower has three petals, three stamens, and three sepals. It blooms in early summer. The sword-like leaves grow in clusters at the bottom. A flag may grow from five inches to three feet. The plant grows from rhizomes, a rootlike system under the ground.

Habitat: **Blue Flags** and **Yellow Flags** grow well in marshes, swamps, and meadows. Many gardeners have established domestic iris beds in their yards.

Gathered: The leaves are the only part of the flag that should be gathered. They can be gathered after the plant has flowered. Most flag gardeners cut the leaves mid-summer so that the majority of the plant's energy will go into the root system.

Storage: The cut leaves should be placed on a drying screen out of the sun in a cool, well-ventilated place. The leaves can also be skirted by using a tapestry needle and strong natural-colored string.

Preparation: Soak the leaves in cool water for approximately 30-45 minutes. Keep them covered in a damp towel. Try to soak only the amount needed for weaving. Re-soaking can cause deterioration of the fiber in the plant. The leaves can also be used in a "green" state although there may be substantial shrinkage.

Comments: Tennessee prizes this beautiful plant so highly it is their state flower. The rhizomes of **Blue Flag** are poisonous and should not be eaten.

Folklore: **Blue Flag** (iris vericolor) was named after the goddess of rainbows whose task was to bring peace after the gods' stormy confrontations. **Yellow Flag** was taken by King Clovis of France as his royal emblem.

flag
IRIS
Blue, Yellow

Flowers: *yellow; or violet blue with yellow, green or white at base of three outer showy sepals ("falls") with 3 erect petals ("standards") and 3 styles (over each sepal) with fussy upturned ends and 3 stamens hidden under the styles.*

Leaves: *long, narrow, swordlike leaves densely clustered at base; 8–32" long.*

Stems: *the underground stem where it attaches to rhizome is flattened and very poisonous.*

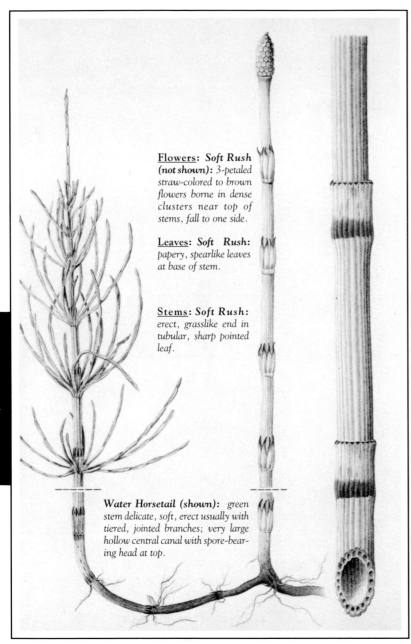

Flowers: *Soft Rush (not shown)*: *3-petaled straw-colored to brown flowers borne in dense clusters near top of stems, fall to one side.*

Leaves: *Soft Rush*: *papery, spearlike leaves at base of stem.*

Stems: *Soft Rush*: *erect, grasslike end in tubular, sharp pointed leaf.*

Water Horsetail *(shown): green stem delicate, soft, erect usually with tiered, jointed branches; very large hollow central canal with spore-bearing head at top.*

rush
JUNCUS/EQUISETUM
Soft Rush, Water Horsetail

Description: Rush is a prehistoric plant with hundreds of species. The upright light green stem will grow from one to several feet high. Some rushes are hollow with many joints. The flower of soft rush grows near the top of the stalk and off to one side. **Water Horsetail** will flower at the tip. Rush can be found growing in clumps.

Habitat: Rushes grow in wet thickets, waste places, marshes, and swamps.

Gathered: Gather rush at the end of summer or early fall after the plant has reached full growth. Carefully cut the rush; never pull rushes out by the roots. This will insure that more stems grow before the next gathering.

Storage: Dry rush on screens, out of the sun. The sun can totally bleach out the color of the stems. Rush can also be bound with cording and hung upside down from beams or drying racks.

Preparation: Fresh rush can be used for weaving. However, shrinkage should be expected. Dried rush should be soaked in water for an hour. Wrap in a damp cloth or towel and keep covered while weaving. Rush can be dried again and used for future weaving.

Comments: Rushes and a variety of grasses have been used for weaving mats, hats, and chair seats.

Folklore: Because of the rough joints in **Horsetail Rush**, it was often broken into smaller sections, bound together and used to scour pots and pans.

Description: The sedge family includes many thousands of species. It is grasslike, usually with a three-cornered stem without nodes. Sedges may grow as little as a few inches to more than 10 feet. The leaves are slender and shorter than the main stalk. Flower-like spikelets form at the top of the plant—a most interesting botanical.

Habitat: Sedges are almost amphibious because of their love for water, growing where many grasses will not grow. Sedges are found in bogs, wet meadows, swamps, shores, and ditches.

Gathered: Sedges are best gathered in late summer or early fall after the plant has reached its full growth. Cut; never pull sedges out by the roots. This will insure more stems growing during the next gathering.

Storage: Dry sedges on a screen out of the sun. The sun can bleach out the color from the materials. Sedge can also be hung in tied bundles from beams or drying racks in a cool, dry, well-ventilated place.

Preparation: Soaked dried sedge in water for a few minutes. Wrap in a damp cloth and "mellow" for 12–24 hours. Too much soaking will darken the plant. Green sedges can be woven into baskets, but expect a great deal of shrinkage.

Comments: Sedges are quite plentiful and in some areas are considered an extremely pesty plant.

Folklore: Some sedges produce small tubular-like roots used in Italian recipes.

ſedge
CAREX
White-topped,
Wool Grass,
Yellow Nut Grass

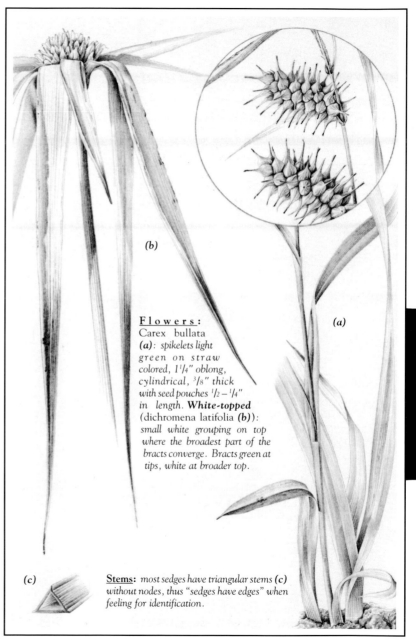

(b)

__Flowers__:
Carex bullata
(a): *spikelets light green on straw colored, 1¼" oblong, cylindrical, ³/₈" thick with seed pouches ½ – ¼" in length.* **White-topped** *(dichromena latifolia* **(b)**)*: small white grouping on top where the broadest part of the bracts converge. Bracts green at tips, white at broader top.*

(a)

(c)

Stems: *most sedges have triangular stems* **(c)** *without nodes, thus "sedges have edges" when feeling for identification.*

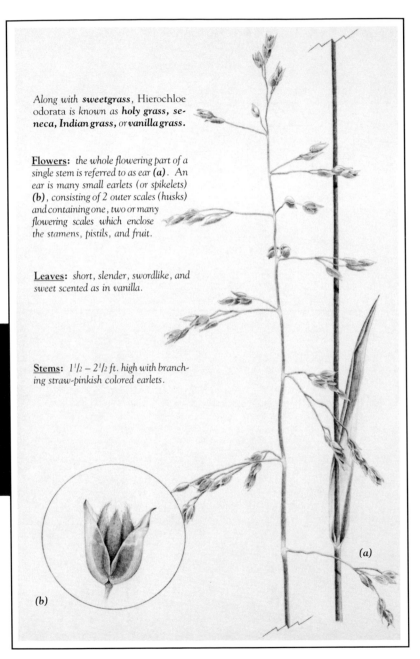

Along with **sweetgrass**, Hierochloe odorata is known as **holy grass, seneca, Indian grass**, or **vanilla grass**.

Flowers: the whole flowering part of a single stem is referred to as ear **(a)**. An ear is many small earlets (or spikelets) **(b)**, consisting of 2 outer scales (husks) and containing one, two or many flowering scales which enclose the stamens, pistils, and fruit.

Leaves: short, slender, swordlike, and sweet scented as in vanilla.

Stems: $1\frac{1}{2} - 2\frac{1}{2}$ ft. high with branching straw-pinkish colored earlets.

(a)

(b)

sweetgrass
HIEROCHLOE ODORATA

Description: Yes, **sweetgrass** is a hard-to-find green grass. It will grow to two and one half feet in one growing season. The main stalk has florets and spikelets. The leaves are slender and spikelike. The grass has very little odor until it is picked. As the plant dries, a pleasing scent emanates. This scent can last for years. It smells like vanilla.

Habitat: Sweetgrass is found in isolated, marshy areas.

Gathered: The grass is gathered in late summer after the plant has reached its full growth. It should be cut close to the ground and never pulled out by the roots.

Storage: Store in a cool, well-ventilated, dry place. Clumps of grass can be bound with cording and hung upside down on a drying rack or beam.

Preparation: "Mellow" in a damp towel overnight and keep covered until weaving. Most **sweetgrass** is used in coiled baskets.

Comments: Sweetgrass bed locations are generally secret, sacred places. This grass can be purchased from isolated nurseries, and beds can be started in yards or gardens.

TREES
ash
elm
maple
oak

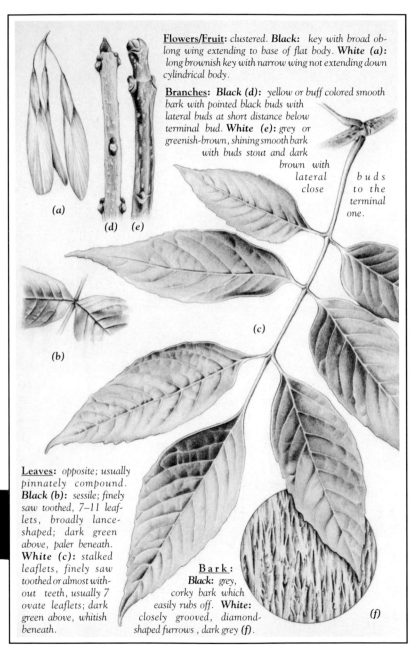

Flowers/Fruit: *clustered.* **Black:** *key with broad oblong wing extending to base of flat body.* **White (a):** *long brownish key with narrow wing not extending down cylindrical body.*

Branches: **Black (d):** *yellow or buff colored smooth bark with pointed black buds with lateral buds at short distance below terminal bud.* **White (e):** *grey or greenish-brown, shining smooth bark with buds stout and dark brown with lateral close buds to the terminal one.*

(a)

(d) (e)

(b)

(c)

Leaves: *opposite; usually pinnately compound.* **Black (b):** *sessile; finely saw toothed, 7–11 leaflets, broadly lance-shaped; dark green above, paler beneath.* **White (c):** *stalked leaflets, finely saw toothed or almost without teeth, usually 7 ovate leaflets; dark green above, whitish beneath.*

Bark: **Black:** *grey, corky bark which easily rubs off.* **White:** *closely grooved, diamond-shaped furrows, dark grey (f).*

(f)

FRAXINUS

Black, Brown, White

Description: The ash family contains many species that grow throughout the United States. **Black, Brown,** and **White Ash** are generally used for basketmaking, with **Black Ash** the predominant tree used. Ash trees grow 30–50 feet, are narrow, and have a rounded crown. The leaves are pinnately compound with 7–11 leaflets. They are lance-shaped and finely toothed. The bark is gray with a broad, oblong, winged fruit which hangs in clusters.

Habitat: Ash grows well in wetlands and swamps. It can be found growing next to conifers and hardwoods.

Gathered: The best time to gather ash is during the spring while there is sap flowing through the cell structure and the pores are larger. Look for a tree seven to nine inches in diameter. The tree should have at least a six-foot section of trunk which is blemish-free.

Storage: Keep the log damp. This can be done by storing in a pond, stream, or burying in the ground or in sawdust. It can also be wrapped in plastic to hold the moisture. Freezing will also preserve the moisture. Store splints in a cool, dry place.

Preparation: Ash must be pounded after the bark is removed. Use a draw knife, knife, ax, or wooden mallet to make splints. For further preparation instructions refer to Richard Schneider's *Crafts of the North American Indians* or to Carol and Dan Hart's *Natural Basketry.*

Comments: Ash is not a sought-after wood. It burns rapidly and is not durable. It is, however, an excellent material for making baskets because it is easily made into splints and will bend without cracking or breaking.

Folklore: The northern Native Americans used all parts (seeds, bark, leaves) for medicinal uses. The bark was used for tea to treat itchy scalps. The seeds were sought for use as an aphrodisiac.

TREES

Description: An elm tree will grow to heights of 70 feet. It has a broad crown and large, rough elliptical, double sawtoothed leaves which have strongly paralleled veins. Elm have one-seeded fruit keys (samara). The samaras mature in spring.

Habitat: Most elm trees grow in moist soils, generally in valleys and flood plains. Elms can also be found on dry uplands.

Gathered: When harvesting elm, look for a straight-trunked tree that has at least a six-foot span free from twigs and knots. The tree should not be larger than four inches in diameter. Harvest any time.

Storage: The log can be made into rims, handles and splints as soon as it is cut. It should be kept damp. This can be done by putting the log in a pond or stream or a canoe filled with water. Wrapping the log in a damp cloth or burlap will also work. Freezing the log is another option. After the splints, rims, and handles are made, keep them in a cool, dry place.

Preparation: The inner bark is the most common part of the tree used. Cut length-wise strips of bark to make splints. Refer to Sue H. Stephenson's *Basketry of the Appalachian Mountains* for proper making of handles, rims and splints. The splints should not be soaked. While weaving, keep splints in a damp towel to prevent cracking and breaking.

Comments: Elm will turn a beautiful brown leathery color after splints have been made. In the 1930's an Asian fungus, Dutch elm disease, was carried from Europe to the United States killing millions of elm trees.

Folklore: North American Indians exposed the inner bark of the elm to water which created a soothing, softening ointment used to treat skin problems.

elm
ULMUS
American, Slippery

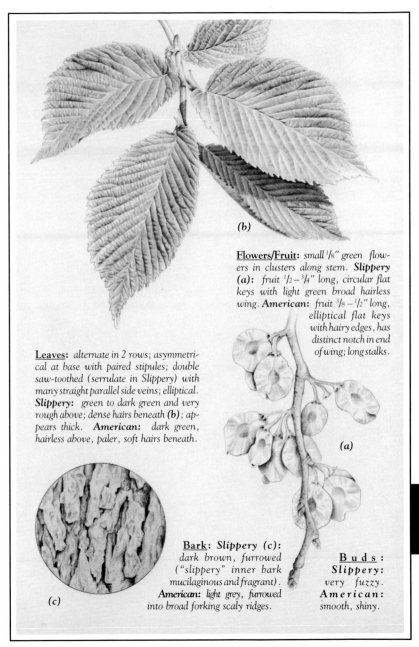

Leaves: *alternate in 2 rows; asymmetrical at base with paired stipules; double saw-toothed (serrulate in Slippery) with many straight parallel side veins; elliptical.* **Slippery:** *green to dark green and very rough above; dense hairs beneath* **(b)**; *appears thick.* **American:** *dark green, hairless above, paler, soft hairs beneath.*

Flowers/Fruit: *small 1/8" green flowers in clusters along stem.* **Slippery (a):** *fruit 1/2 – 3/4" long, circular flat keys with light green broad hairless wing.* **American:** *fruit 3/8 – 1/2" long, elliptical flat keys with hairy edges, has distinct notch in end of wing; long stalks.*

Bark: Slippery (c): *dark brown, furrowed ("slippery" inner bark mucilaginous and fragrant).* **American:** *light grey, furrowed into broad forking scaly ridges.*

Buds: Slippery: *very fuzzy.* **American:** *smooth, shiny.*

TREES

35

maple
ACER
Sugar

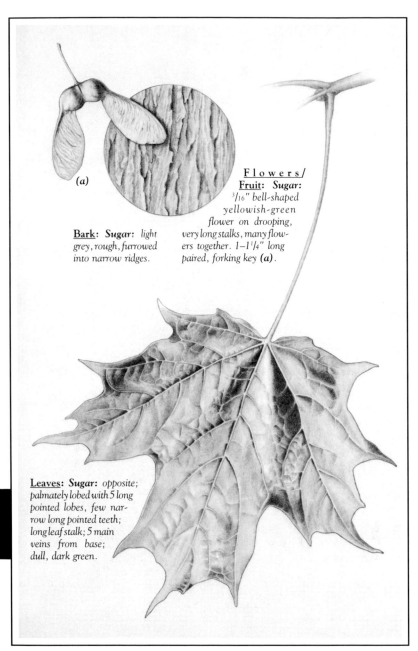

(a)

Bark: *Sugar: light grey, rough, furrowed into narrow ridges.*

Flowers/ Fruit: *Sugar: ³/₁₆" bell-shaped yellowish-green flower on drooping, very long stalks, many flowers together. 1–1¹/₄" long paired, forking key* **(a)**.

Leaves: *Sugar: opposite; palmately lobed with 5 long pointed lobes, few narrow long pointed teeth; long leaf stalk; 5 main veins from base; dull, dark green.*

TREES

Description: **Sugar Maple** grows primarily in the upper Midwest, eastern states and Canada. It is a large tree, growing 70–100 feet, and has a rounded crown. The leaves are a dark green with five large main lobes and have a few smaller notched teeth along the edge. The leaves turn brilliant reds, yellows, and oranges in the fall. The bark is gray and the fruit seed key is called a samara. The samaras have paired wings and spin as they fall to the ground.

Habitat: Maple grows best in rich valleys and uplands. Many people plant this fast growing tree in their yards for shade.

Gathered: Gather maple anytime during the year. Choose a tree no more than four inches in diameter with a blemish-free trunk that is at least six feet long.

Storage: The maple log should be kept damp by placing it in water (a pond or a trough) or burying it in sawdust. The log should not be allowed to dry out. It can also be placed in a freezer. Store splints in a cool, dry place.

Preparation: Maple can be made into splints using an ax, wedges, froes, and a knife. Refer to Jim Bennett's *Handling White Oak* or Sue H. Stephenson's *Basketry of the Appalachian Mountains* for proper making of handles, rims and splints. Wrap dried splints in a damp towel for more flexible weaving without cracking or breaking. Splints should never be soaked. If working with fresh materials, some shrinkage can be expected.

Comments: The Canadians revere the maple tree so highly they chose it for their national emblem.

Folklore: In spring the **Sugar Maple** tree produces sap. Sap is collected and boiled down into syrups and sugars. With the onset of warm days and cool nights, one **Sugar Maple** will yield 5-60 gallons of sap each season. The length of time it can be collected will vary from year to year. It will take about 32 gallons of sap to produce one gallon of syrup. If boiled down further, the sap will produce four and one half pounds of the type of sugar early settlers used as brown sugar in recipes and treats.

Description: **White Oak** is one of the largest North American trees. It can grow to 100 feet. The crown of the tree is rounded. The obovate leaf is a bright green color, has five to nine lobes, a short stem, and bears fruit called acorns. The acorns are encased in a scaly cap and turn brown with maturity. The bark is gray. A **White Oak** tree will hold its leaves throughout the winter.

Habitat: The habitat for **White Oak** will range from river-banks to hillsides.

Gathered: **White Oak** can be gathered year-round. The basketmaker should look for a tree which is four to eight inches in diameter. The tree should have a straight five to six foot midsection which has no twigs or branches. Look for straight ridges on the bark.

Storage: The log should be cut into handles, rims or splints within three to four days. The log can rest for as long as five months. Some basketmakers store the log in sawdust to retain its moisture and others freeze the log. After the handles, rims, and splints are formed, they should be stored in a cool, dry place to prevent mildew.

Preparation: Preparing **White Oak** is an involved process using an ax, wedges, froes and knives. One should refer to Jim Bennett's *Handling White Oak* or Sue H. Stephenson's *Basketry of the Appalachian Mountains* for detailed information concerning the splinting of **White Oak**. This method of splint making can also be applied to sassafras.

Comments: A used basket made of **White Oak** can exist 50 to 70 years or more. Over half of all wood used for furniture in the United States is oak.

Folklore: The Native Americans had a multitude of uses for oak. Acorns were used after drying and grinding into find meal for cornmeals and breads. The bark was simmered in water and had wide medicinal uses. Fine whiskies and sherries are aged in **White Oak** barrels.

oak
QUERCUS
White

Flowers/Fruit: White: *acorn is egg shaped, with shallow cup of knobby scales turning light grey, maturing first year.*

Bark: White: *smooth and blunt buds (all oaks have clusters of buds at ends of branchlets); light grey in broad plates or ridges which often break loose.*

Leaves: White: *simple; obovate with 5–9 rounded lobes, deep sinus sometimes to midrib, widest beyond middle with tapering to base; bright green surface, grey-green beneath; hairless; often remaining on tree in winter.*

TREES

OTHERS
catalpa
corn
pine
roots
sumac
38

Description: Northern Catalpa is a large tree reaching heights of 80 feet. The top of the tee is very rounded and the branches are far spreading, making a perfect shade tree. The leaves are heart-shaped, not toothed, and are quite large. In late spring a bell-shaped white flower develops. From the flower, a long (8–18 inches), narrow, slender pod forms. In late fall this pod will turn a dark brown

Habitat: Catalpa is a domesticated tree generally grown in yards. It is seldom seen growing in the wild.

Gathered: In spring, the catalpa pod will split open and fall from the branches. It can then be gathered from the ground in "basketfulls."

Storage: Store the dried pods in a tied bundle or in a paper bag. Keep in a dry, cool place until ready to weave.

Preparation: First split the pods open and remove seeds if necessary. This can easily be done with an awl or a pocket knife. Soak pods in warm water for at least an hour before weaving. Drain well and keep wrapped in a damp towel. The unused pods can be dried and soaked again.

Comments: Catalpa pods make excellent decorative objects for the home. Place a gathering of pods in a basket for a natural bouquet.

Folklore: The Cherokee Indians named the catalpa tree. It was called "Indian-Bean" tree because of its distinctive fruit.

catalpa
CATALPA
Common Catalpa Pods
Nothern Catalpa Pods

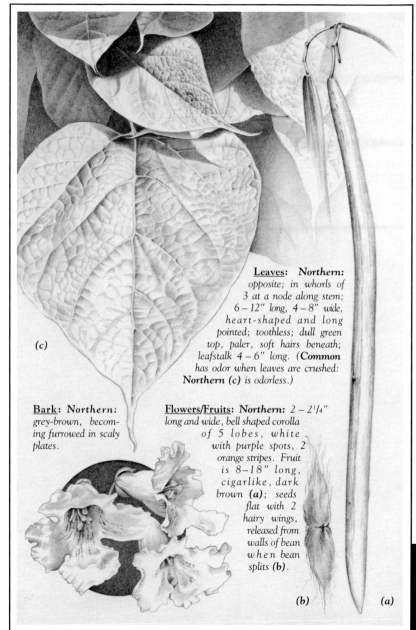

(c)

Leaves: *Northern: opposite; in whorls of 3 at a node along stem; 6 – 12" long, 4 – 8" wide, heart-shaped and long pointed; toothless; dull green top, paler, soft hairs beneath; leafstalk 4 – 6" long. (**Common** has odor when leaves are crushed: **Northern (c)** is odorless.)*

Bark: Northern: *grey-brown, becoming furrowed in scaly plates.*

Flowers/Fruits: Northern: *2 – 2¼" long and wide, bell shaped corolla of 5 lobes, white with purple spots, 2 orange stripes. Fruit is 8–18" long, cigarlike, dark brown (**a**); seeds flat with 2 hairy wings, released from walls of bean when bean splits (**b**).*

(b)   (a)

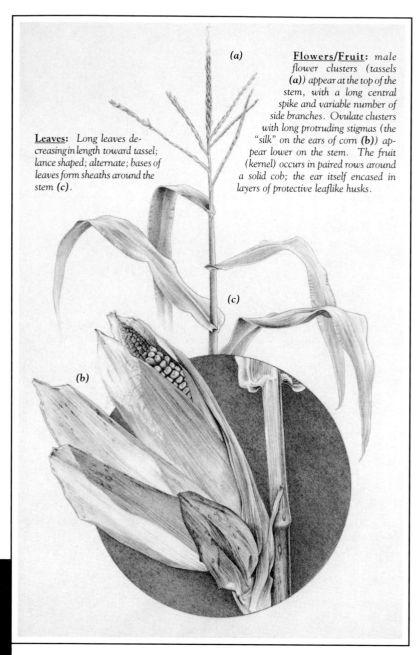

Leaves: *Long leaves decreasing in length toward tassel; lance shaped; alternate; bases of leaves form sheaths around the stem (c).*

Flowers/Fruit: *male flower clusters (tassels (a)) appear at the top of the stem, with a long central spike and variable number of side branches. Ovulate clusters with long protruding stigmas (the "silk" on the ears of corn (b)) appear lower on the stem. The fruit (kernel) occurs in paired rows around a solid cob; the ear itself encased in layers of protective leaflike husks.*

Corn
ZEA
Corn Husks

Description: Corn is most easily distinguished by its ears, long leaves, and tassels appearing on the top of the stems. An ear always has an even number of rows of kernals, and most field corn kernals appear to be "dented" on the visible surface.

Habitat: Corn is grown in cultivated fields and gardens throughout the Americas.

Gathered: Collect corn husks after the plants have reached full maturity. Gathering can be done as early as July with sweet corn through late October with field corn.

Storage: Dry fresh corn husks on a screen or newspaper. They will retain a light green hue if dried out of the sun. Corn husks can be easily lightened with liquid household bleach. The husks absorb dyes readily and will accept a wide range of colors. Store in paper bags in a cool, dry, well-ventilated place.

Preparation: Corn husks can be torn into strips and soaked in water for an hour. Wrap in a damp towel and "mellow" overnight. Keep covered while using.

Comments: Husks can be twisted, braided, made into cordage or woven successfully.

Folklore: If a family could not afford ticking feather for a mattress, corn husks were often used.

Description: The pines, also known as conifers, grow in many shapes and sizes with varied lengths of needles. The longest needle species are the best for basketmaking. **White Pine (*pinus strobus*) and Longleaf Pine (*pinus palustris*)** are two trees with needles growing in clusters from 6–18 inches long. These trees can grow to heights of 100 feet or more. They grow slowly and can be found in almost pure stands. The bark is gray and deeply cracked. The pines generally produce four to ten inch brown cones which bear fruit with seeds in two seasons.

Habitat: Pines grow best in sandy soil, but can be found growing in wet bogs and dry ridges.

Gathered: Pine needles can be gathered anytime. The basketmaker can collect needles that have already fallen from the trees. Needles also can be carefully pulled off the trees.

Storage: Green needles can be dried on screens in or out of the sun depending on the color desired. The needles should first be washed gently in detergent and water. Store in a paper bag or wrap bundles in newspaper. Store in a cool, dry place.

Preparation: Pine needles, if not flexible, can be soaked in water for 30 minutes and wrapped in a towel. Mellow overnight for best results. Some needles do not have to be soaked before using. Refer to Judy Mulford's *Basic Pine Needle Basketry* for more details on working with pine needles.

Comments: The pine tree is Maine's state tree. It has a very durable wood used in the construction of homes. **Longleaf Pines** are tapped for turpentine.

Folklore: The pines are a most vital group of edible wild plants. Many parts of the tree are milled, baked and even boiled. The Adirondacks is an Indian name for "tree-eaters." **White Pines** grow so densely in the northern parts of the United States that pioneers declared squirrels could travel a lifetime without coming out of the trees.

pine
PINUS
Longleaf Pine Needles
White Pine Needles

Fruit: *cones usually mature in 2 years, opening to disperse winged seeds.* **White (a):** *4–8" cones, yellow-brown when immature, thin flattened cone scales with minute prickle.* **Longleaf (b):** *6–10" cones, dull brown when immature with raised cone scales that each have a small prickle.*

Leaves (needles): *evergreen, in clusters.* **White (a):** *3 – 6" in grouping of 5, not sheathed at base (c); blue-green.* **Longleaf (b):** *6" and longer in grouping of 3, dense bundles, dark green.*

Bark: *grey and rough on young trees to furrowed scaly plates on mature (orangish-brown in mature* **Longleaf***).*

(a) *(c)* *(b)*

41

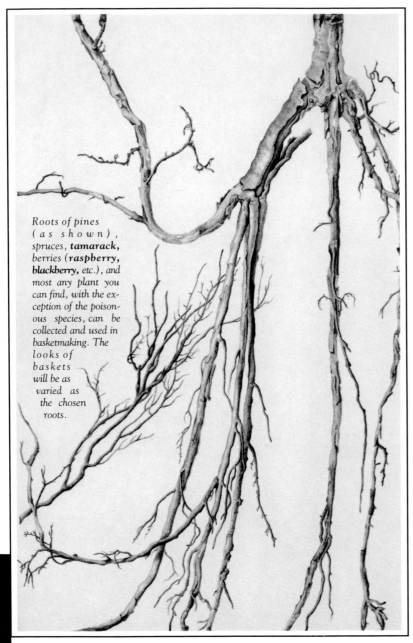

*Roots of pines (as shown), spruces, **tamarack,** berries (**raspberry, blackberry,** etc.), and most any plant you can find, with the exception of the poisonous species, can be collected and used in basketmaking. The looks of baskets will be as varied as the chosen roots.*

Description: Roots anchor plants and trees into the soil. The roots also transport needed nutrients to the plant and store food. **Black Spruce, Jack Pine, Tamarack,** and varied other roots are used in basketmaking.

Habitat: Many exposed roots can be found along riverbeds, streams, beaches, and inland seas. Roots can also be located on excavation sites such as new roads and residential building sites.

Gathered: Roots can be found from spring through summer or early fall before the ground freezes. Only collect two to three root lengths from each tree. Pulling too many roots from one plant can destroy the tree.

Storage: Roots should be prepared soon after gathering. After preparing, store in coils in a cool, dry place and off the floor to discourage pest and bugs.

Preparation: After collecting roots, soak them in water for a day or more. Using a knife, remove the bark. Large roots can be split and coiled for later use. Dried roots need to be soaked for a day or until they are flexible. Dick Schneider's *Crafts of the North American Indians* can be used as a reference when working with spruce roots.

Comments: Alaskan Eskimos gather cedar roots for basketmaking in the spring and place them in a fire for a few minutes to remove the bark. Many roots contain nutritional and medicinal qualities; other roots are extremely poisonous.

Folklore: Doug Elliot says that Fra Tomás de Berlana in1420 suggested that root vegetation is simply animal life turned inside out. Medicine men and women used roots to conjure treatments for curing baldness, colds, toothaches, and insomnia.

OTHERS

Description: Sumac is a small tree or tall bush growing in thickets. It is the only tree native to all contiguous states. The long, pinnately compound central leaf stalk has many sawtoothed leaves. The bark is a dark brown and can be smooth or scaly. **Staghorn Sumac** has a velvety covering. In late summer, sumac will produce a long, dark red, hairy fruit with clusters of berries. When the twigs are cut, a gummy white sap appears.

Habitat: Sumac grows well along roadsides, old fields, and at edges of woods. It will not grow in the shade.

Gathered: The center leafstalks can be gathered during the summer, but the leaves must be removed. If gathered in the fall, the brilliant red color will remain on the stalk.

Storage: Store leafstalks in a bundle rolled into a newspaper or in a paper bag. Place in a cool, dry, well-ventilated storage area.

Preparation: Place leafstalks in cool water for 30-40 minutes. Drain well and roll them into a damp towel.

Comments: Caution must be taken not to gather poison sumac. It can be identified by white drooping berry clusters. It will not have the red berry stalk.

Folklore: "Indian lemonade" can be made by gathering the **Staghorn Sumac's** red berry stalks in late summer. Place the stalks in a container of boiling water and steep. Drain the mixture through a couple of layers of cheesecloth to remove debris. A sweetener can be added to the juice for a thirst-quenching cooler.

Sumac
RHUS
Shining or Dwarf
Smooth, Staghorn

Flowers/Fruit: *clusters of male flowers yellow, clusters of female flowers greenish at first turning red; terminal (**Poison Sumac** and **Poison Ivy** are found along stems and have white fruit.) **Staghorn:** fuzzy red berrylike (1/8") in clusters with long sticky red hairs. **Smooth (a):** fruit as in **Staghorn** but short hairs.*

(b)

(a)

Branchlets: **Staghorn:** *hairy and brown like stag's antlers.* **Smooth (b):** *smooth with lenticels more obvious on mature; glaucous.*

Leaves: *alternate; 12" long with 11–30 leaflets; green above, velvety, hairy.* **Shining** *or midrib appearing as very* *pinnately 2–4" lancewhitish beneath.* **Dwarf:** *leaves with wide flattened stem.* *compound; leaves shaped, serrated* **Staghorn:** *densely "wings" down entire*

OTHERS

43

GLOSSARY[1]

Alternate. Not opposite; only one leaf or bud at a node.

Axil. Angle, as in the angle where a leaf meets a stem.

Axillary. Situated in an axil.

Bract. A small leaf or scale, in the axil of which a flower, cluster, or cone scale may be borne.

Branchlet. The growth of the last season on any stem.

Bud. An undeveloped stem with undeveloped leaves and/or flowers.

Bud scales. Small, dry, modified leaves covering a bud.

Calyx. A collective name for the sepals.

Catkin. A spike of unisexual flowers (compacted and drooping often, as in later stage on the branches of willow).

Ciliate. Fringed with hairs.

Compound leaf. A leaf whose blade is divided into separate parts called leaflets.

Cone. A spikelike cluster of scales bearing naked seeds.

Connate. Grown together.

Cordate. Heart-shaped at the base (as in leaves).

Corolla. Collective name for the petals.

Crenate. Scalloped, or with rounded teeth.

Cuneate. Wedge-shaped at base.

Elliptic. About twice as long as wide, with the general outline of an ellipse, the two ends about the same width.

Entire. With an even margin, not toothed, or divided.

Evergreen. Remaining green through the winter.

Fruit. A ripened ovary or seed vessel.

Glaucous. Covered with white or bluish bloom which rubs off, as on grapes.

Green. A live cut plant or branch not prepared or dried.

Internode. The part of the stem between two nodes.

Lanceolate. Shaped as a lance—longer than wide, tapering to a point at the upper end, and slightly narrowed at the base.

Lateral. Situated on the side.

Leaflet. One of the parts of a compound leaf, small leaf on mainstalk.

Leafstalk. The stem of a leaf.

Lenticel. A raised dot marking a region of loose aerating tissue in bark.

Linear. Long a very narrow, with parallel margins.

Lobe. A segment of a leaf whose margin is too deeply cut to be called toothed.

Mellowed. A method of softening fiber in a plant, usually done by wrapping the plant in a damp towel overnight.

Midrib. The central vein of a leaf.

Mucilaginous. The nature of being gummy or secreting substances.

Needle. A long, slender, more or less needle-shaped leaf.

Node. A place on the stem where one or more leaves grow.

1 Many entries from Arthur Harmount Graves, *Illustrated Guide to Trees and Shrubs,* New York, New York: Harper & Row Publishers, Inc., 1952.

44

Nut. A hard, mostly one-seeded, fruit that does not split open when ripe.

Oblong. Longer than wide, with margins nearly parallel.

Obovate. Ovate with the narrow end toward the base.

Opposite. Two leaves or buds at a node occuring on opposite sides of the stem at the same level.

Oval. Broadly elliptical, less than twice as long as wide.

Ovate. Egg-shaped with the wider end toward the base.

Palmate. Resembling a hand. Palmately-lobed, with sinuses pointing toward the petiole; palmately-compound, with leaflets all attached to the tip of the petiole.

Pendulous. Drooping.

Petal. One of the modified leaves forming the inner circle of leaflike parts of a flower, next to and surrounding the stamens.

Petiole. The stalk of a leaf.

Pinnate. Resembling a feather.

Pistil. Central organ of a flower, in the base (ovary) where seeds form.

Pith. The softer, central part of a stem.

Prickle. A slender, sharp-pointed outgrowth from the young bark or epidermis.

Rhombic. With 4 nearly equal sides, but not rectangular.

Samara. A winged fruit; key.

Scale. A very small leaf, often dry; a tiny flattened outgrowth found on the epidermis; a flake of bark.

Serrate. Saw-toothed; with sharp teeth pointing forward.

Serrulate. Finely toothed.

Sessile. Without a stalk.

Shoot. Stem and leaves.

Simple. Not branched...not compound.

Sinus. The indentation between two lobes.

Spike. A cluster of sessile flowers borne close together on a elongated axis; an elongated flower cluster as that growing at the tip of sedges.

Stamen. One of the pollen-bearing organs of a flower.

Stem. The trunk, branch, branchlet, or twig of the plant; not the stalk of the leaf, which is the petiole.

Stipules. Small appendages occurring in pairs at the bases of the petioles of the leaves of certain plants.

Style. The usually slender upper part of the pistil connecting stigma and ovary.

Tendril. Thread-like organ as stem or leaf part which coils around or is fastened to a support (fences, walls, trees).

Thickets. Bushes, shrubs or small trees growing in dense patches.

Toothed. Short projections between shallow notches on the margin of a leaf.

Twig. A small branch, usually including several years' growth.

Uplands. High land.

Veins. Strands of conducting tissue forming the framework of leaves.

Whorl. A circle of three or more (leaves or buds) around the stem.

Wing. A thin expansion of, or appendage to, an organ.

BIBLIOGRAPHY

Angier, Bradford. *Field Guide to Edible Wild Plants,* 1974.   Stackpole Books. Cameron and Kelker Streets, Harrisburg, Pennsylvania 17105. ----------*Field Guide to Medicinal Wild Plants,* 1978.   Stackpole Books.

Baker, Arthur.   *Calligraphy, 1973.* Dover Publications, Inc., New York, New York.

Bates, Kenneth S.   *Baskets,* circular 527.   Cooperative Extension Service, University of Arkansas, Department of Agriculture, and U.S. Department of Agriculture, cooperating.

Bennett, Jim.   *Handling White Oak,* 1974.   Deer Track Crafts. 8215 Beeman Road, Chelsea, Michigan 48118.

Bliss, Anne.   *Weeds: A Guide for Dyers,* 1978.   Juniper House. P.O. Box 2094, Boulder Colorado 80306.

Brown, Lauren.   *The Audobon Society Nature—Grasslands,* 1947.   Alfred A. Knopf, Inc., New York, New York. ----------*Weeds in Winter,* 1986.   W.W. Norton & Co., Inc., New York, New York.

Buckles, Mary Parker and Carter Harmon.   *The Flowers Around Us,* 1985.   University of Missouri Press, Columbia, Missouri   65211.

Cutler, Karen Davis.   "Divine Climbers," *Harrowsmith,* Jan./Feb. 1988, pp.66-72.   Camden House Publishing House, Inc., The Creamery, Charlotte, Vermont 05445.

Daugherty, Robin Tayler.   *Splint Woven Basketry,* 1986.   Interweave Press, 306 North Washington Avenue, Loveland, Colorado   80537.

Dowden, Anne Ophelia.   *From Flower to Fruit,* 1984.   Thomas Y. Crowell, New York, New York.

Durrell, Gerald.   *A Practical Guide for the Amateur Naturalist,* 1986.   Alfred A. Knopf, New York, New York.

Edsall, Marian S.   *Roadside Plants and Flowers: A Traveler's Guide to the Midwest and Great Lakes Area,* 1985.   The University of Wisconsin Press, 114 North Murray Street, Madison, Wisconsin   53715.

Elliott, Doug.   *Woodslore and Wildwoods Wisdom,* 1986.   Possum Productions, Route 4, Box 137, Burnsvile, North Carolina   28714.

Graves, Arthur Harmount.   *Illustrated Guide to Trees and Shrubs,* 1952.   Harper & Row Publishers, Inc., 49 East 33rd Street, New York, New York.

Hart, Carol and Dan.   *Natural Basketry,* 1976.   Watson-Guptill Publications, 1515 Broadway, New York, New York   10036.

James, George Wharton.   *Indian Basketry,* 1909.   Dover Publications, Inc., 180 Varick Street, New York, New York   10014.

Knobel, Edward.   *Field Guide to the Grasses, Sedges and Rushes of the United States,* 1977.   Dover Publications, Inc., 180 Varick Street, New York, New York   10014.

Lasansky, Jeannette.   *Willow, Oak and Rye,* 1979.   The Pennsylvania State University, 215 Wagner Building, University Park, Pennsylvania   16802.

Little, Elbert L.   *The Audobon Society Field Guide to North American Trees,* 1980.   Alfred A. Knopf, Inc., New York, New York.

Madsen, John.   "Trees that Weep, Whistle, and Grow Kittens," *Audubon,* September, 1985, pp. 44-57.   950 Third Avenue, New York, New York.

Meilach, Dona, and Dee Menagh.   *Basketry Today with Materials from Nature,* 1979.   Crown Publishers, Inc., One Park Avenue, New York, New York   10016.

Mulford, Judy.   *Basic Pine Needle Basketry,* 1986.   Judy Mulford, 2098 Mandeville Canyon Road, Los Angeles, California   90049.

Neiring, William A.   *The Audobon Society Field Guide to North American Wildflowers,* 1979.   Alfred A. Knopf, Inc., New York, New York.
----------- *The Audubon Nature Guides – Wetlands,* 1924.   Alfred A Knopf, Inc., New York, New York.

Phillips, Roger.   *Trees of North America and Europe,* 1978.   Random House, Inc., New York, New York.

Raven, Peter H., Ray F. Evert and Susan E. Eichhorn.   *Biology of Plants,* Fourth Ed., 1986.   Worth Publishers, Inc., New York, New York.

Reader's Digest.   *Magic and Medicine of Plants,* 1986.   Reader's Digest, New York, New York.
----------- *North American Wildlife,* 1982.   New York, New York.

Riotte, Louise.   *Sleeping with a Sunflower,* 1987.   Storey Communications, Inc., Schoolhouse Road, Pownal, Vermont   05261.

Schanz, Joanna E.   *Willow Basketry of the Amana Colonies,* 1986.   Schanz Broom and Basket Shop, West Amana, Iowa   52357.

Schneider, Richard C.   *Crafts of the North American Indians,* 1972.   Van Nostrand Reinhold Co., 450 West 33rd Street, New York, New York   10001.

Smith Sue M.   *Natural Fiber Basketry,* 1983.   Willow Bend Press, 3544 Hilltop Road, Fort Worth, Texas   76109.

Sorden, L.G., and Robert Gard.   *Wisconsin Lore,* 1976.   Stanton & Lee Publishers, Sauk City, Wisconsin   53583.

Spencer, Edwin Rollin.   *All About Weeds,* 1940.   Dover Publications, Inc., 180 Varick Street, New York, New York   10014.

Stephenson, Sue H.   *Basketry of the Appalachian Mountains,* 1977.   Van Nostrand Reinhold Co., 450 West 33rd Street, New York, New York   10001.

Strom, John.   *Lawns, Trees and Shrubs.* 1961.   Golden Press, New York, New York.

Symonds, George W.   *The Shrub Identification Book,* 1963.   William Morrow & Company, Inc., New York, New York.
----------- *The Tree Identification Book,* 1958.   William Morrow & Company, New York, New York.

Tatum, Billy Joe.   *Wild Foods Field Guide and Cookbook,* 1976.   Workman Publishing Co., Inc., 1 West 39th Street, New York, New York   10018.

Taylor's Guide to Ground Covers, Vines & Grasses, 1961.   Chanticleer Press, Inc., New York, New York.

Taylor's Guide to Shrubs, 1961.   Chanticleer Press, Inc.

TerBeest, Char.   *Wisconsin Willow – Adventures of a Basketmaker,* 1985.   Wild Willow Press, P.O. Box 438, Baraboo, Wisconsin   53913.

Trelease, William.   *Winter Botany – An Identification Guide to Native Trees and Shrubs,* 1918.   Dover Publications, Inc., 184 Varick Street, New York, New York   10014.

Webster, Sandy.   *A Handbook (Naturally) to Basketry,* 1986.

Weiner, Michael A.   *Earth Medicines – Earth Foods,* 1972.   Macmillian Publishing Co., Inc., 866 Third Avenue, New York, New York.

Wigginton, Eliot.   *The Foxfire Book,* 1986.   Anchor Press/Doubleday, Garden City, New York.

Whitman, Ann H.   *Familiar Trees of North America,* 1986.   Alfred A. Knopf, Inc., New York, New York.

Wild Willow Press / Ampersand